*The Employee Handbook of*

# NEW WORK HABITS FOR A RADICALLY CHANGING WORLD

## Price Pritchett

*13 Ground Rules for Job Success In the Information Age*

PRITCHETT & ASSOCIATES, INC.
Dallas, Texas

*During the early 1900's, 85% of our workers were in agriculture. Now agriculture involves less than 3% of the workforce.*

*In 1950, 73% of U.S. employees worked in production or manufacturing. Now less than 15% do.*

*The Department of Labor estimates that by the year 2000 at least 44% of all workers will be in data services—for example, gathering, processing, retrieving, or analyzing information.*

*Careers come and go. Jobs change. This is nothing new – it's just happening far faster than ever before.*

You're involved in something *BIG:* The shift to an entirely new economy...a new age...a vastly different approach in the way organizations operate.

Work is going global. We're entering the Information Age. The economy is shifting more and more toward *services,* and toward *knowledge work.* Before long, top management absolutely won't be able to run things the old way, even if it desperately wants to.

New technologies—especially computers and telecommunications—have already created intense, worldwide competition for business. Soon, competition for your very own job could come from practically anywhere on earth.

Careers have already quit working like they used to. That's not really *anybody's* fault. But employees and organizations are very much at fault if they, too, don't change in order to adapt.

It does us no good whatsoever to complain or be bitter about what's happening. In fact, such behavior can only do us harm. We waste precious energy if we resist, get angry, or give in to grief over all that's being lost. We jeopardize our future if we cling to old assumptions and expectations about how careers should operate.

Frankly, the world doesn't care about our opinions. Or our feelings. The world rewards only those of us who catch on to what's happening, who invest our energy in finding and seizing the opportunities brought about by change.

And change *always* comes bearing gifts.

Considering the scope and speed of change these days, there will be precious gifts—many priceless opportunities—for those of us who play by the new rules, position ourselves right, and take personal responsibility for our future.

*Meet the challenge.* Follow these 13 guidelines for managing your job during radical change.

PRITCHETT & ASSOCIATES, INC.
*Dallas, Texas*

# Table of Contents

*As recently as the 1960's, almost one-half of all workers in the industrialized countries were involved in making (or helping to make) things.*

*By the year 2000, however, no developed country will have more than one-sixth or one-eighth of its workforce in the traditional roles of making and moving goods.*

*Already an estimated two-thirds of U.S. employees work in the* services *sector, and "knowledge" is becoming our most important "product."*

*This calls for different organizations, as well as different kinds of workers.*

– Peter F. Drucker,
*Post-Capitalist Society*

## *Become a quick-change artist.*

**T**aking care of your career these days means managing perpetual motion.

Your organization will keep reshaping itself, shifting and flexing to fit our rapidly changing world. That's the *only* way it can hope to survive in this fiercely competitive environment. Look for it to restructure, outsource, downsize, subcontract, and form new alliances.

You also can expect flexible ways of working. Duties will be constantly realigned. Short-lived assignments will be common. Maybe you'll work on a contract basis, or spend time on several project teams. You might even end up working for more than one "employer" at a time. You'll probably have a constantly new set of coworkers, more new bosses, even new careers.

You're not going to like some of this. Chances are, nobody will like it *all.* But that's neither here nor there. Question is, will you get with the program anyhow?

You need to know that resistance to change is almost always a dead-end street. The career opportunities come when you align immediately with new organizational needs and realities. When you're light on your feet. When you show high capacity for adjustment. Organizations want people who adapt–*fast*–not those who resist or psychologically "unplug."

Granted, change can be painful. When it damages careers, emotions such as grief, anger, and depression come naturally, making it hard for people to "buy in" and be productive. But being a quick-change artist can build your reputation, while resisting change can ruin it. Mobility, not mourning, makes you a valuable member of the group.

Shoot for rapid recovery. Instant alignment.

Take personal responsibility for adapting to change, just like you would if you accepted a new job with a new employer.

*"You think you understand the situation, but what you don't understand is that the situation just changed."*

– Putnam Investments advertisement

*In 1991, for the first time ever, companies spent more money on computing and communications gear than the combined monies spent on industrial, mining, farm, and construction equipment.*

*This spending pattern offers hard proof that we have entered a new era.*

*The Industrial Age has given way to the Information Age.*

## *Commit fully to your job.*

Expect your employer to expect more from you. The reason? The marketplace is demanding far more these days from the organization itself.

Clients and customers want much better quality than before. They expect top-notch service, too, or they'll take their business to your competitors. Speed is also essential, because people have gotten used to instant everything. Frankly, the only way your organization can even hope to compete is to employ high performance people. In times past, the most common solution to problems was just to hire more employees. Spend more money. But companies can't afford that approach any more. Instead of simply throwing more people at problems, organizations now throw fewer. They have to do more—faster and better—with less. This calls for highly committed people.

There's no room now for employees who mainly put in their time, going through the motions but giving only half-hearted effort. The people who seemed to keep their jobs merely because they could "fog the mirror" are goners.

In today's world, career success belongs to the committed. To those who work from the heart...who invest themselves passionately in their jobs...and who *recommit* quickly when change reshapes their work.

If you find you can't recommit rapidly when the company changes, you probably should quit. Get out of there. Don't waste your energy resisting change, and don't kill precious time sitting on the fence. Either buy in, or be on your way, because that's best for both you and your employer.

This is not the same as asking that you be "loyal" to the organization. That would probably strike you as rather hypocritical anyhow, because we've all seen that the world puts hard limits on how loyal an employer can be in return. But urging you to have high job commitment actually serves your best interests, even as it benefits the company.

Strong job commitment makes work far more satisfying. It's therapeutic, too, an excellent antidote for stress and a fine cure for the pain of change. It also empowers you, bringing out your very best potential, and making you a more valuable employee.

Bottom line: Commitment is a gift you should give to yourself.

*"They're only puttin'
in a nickel, but they
want a dollar song."*

– Song title

*You're in Paris, and you decide to use your American Express card. Getting credit approval involves a 46,000-mile journey over phones and computers.*

*The job can be completed in 5 seconds.*

– Peter Large

*The Micro Revolution Revisited*

## *Speed up.*

Examine the corporate body count over the last dozen years or so. What you'll find is that "slow" kills companies. And that, of course, means the death of many careers.

To survive–certainly to gain any competitive advantage–your organization must travel light and cover ground quicker. That drives the decision to decentralize, to delegate decision-making power. That's why it's important to erase boundaries between different parts of the organization, so work flows seamlessly and swiftly. Organizations really don't have much choice. They must eliminate excess baggage…abandon bureaucratic practices…shrink, dramatically, the time it takes to get things done.

So many of the changes you see going on these days are designed to help organizations pick up speed. These are not casual moves or random acts dreamed up by bored and heartless top executives. What you're witnessing are raw survival instincts at work. Organizations *must* accelerate, or they will die.

We live in an impatient world, with fierce competition and fleeting opportunities. Organizations that are lean, agile, and quick to respond clearly have the edge.

But organizations can't go fast if their employees go slow.

So you need to operate with a strong sense of urgency. Accelerate in all aspects of your work, even if it means living with a few more ragged edges. Emphasize *action*. Don't bog down in endless preparation trying to get things perfect before you make a move. Sure, high quality is crucial, but it must come quickly. You can't sacrifice speed. Learn to fail fast, fix it, and race on. Seek radical breakthroughs–quantum leaps– rather than relying solely on incremental, step-by-step improvements.

Take no part whatsoever in resistance to change. If the organization decides to turn on a dime, follow it like a trailer. Corner quickly. Turn for turn. The organization can't wait for employees to go through some slow adjustment process. It can't afford to gear down while people decide whether or not they're going to get on board.

Consider this: New hires join up ready and willing to help drive the organization in new directions. They're eager to prove themselves and make their mark. You would be that same way if you left your present job and hired on with a different outfit. So why not take that approach right where you are? Now.

Instead of being a drag on change initiatives–one of the resisters who causes delay–develop a reputation as one who pushes the change process along. Make yourself more valuable. Help create a high-velocity operation.

*"I have a microwave fireplace. You can lay down in front of the fire all night in eight minutes."*
– Steven Wright

*Since 1983, the U.S. work world has added 25,000,000 computers. The number of cellular telephone subscribers has jumped from zero in 1983 to 16,000,000 by the end of 1993.*

*Close to 19,000,000 people now carry pagers, and almost 12,000,000,000 messages were left in voice mailboxes in 1993 alone.*

*Since 1987, homes and offices have added 10,000,000 fax machines, while E-mail addresses have increased by over 26,000,000.*

*Communication technology is radically changing the speed, direction, and amount of information flow, even as it alters work roles all across organizations. As a case in point, the number of secretaries is down 521,000 just since 1987.*

– Rich Tetzeli,
"Surviving Information Overload"
*Fortune,* July 11, 1994

## *Accept ambiguity and uncertainty.*

**P**inning down your job during change can be like trying to nail Jell-O to the wall.

You're faced with new expectations, shifting priorities, and different reporting relationships. Your role may be vaguely defined, and your assignments may get altered constantly. Usually there are more questions than there are answers.

People who have a high need for structure simply hate this kind of situation. After a while it even eats on employees who have a high tolerance for ambiguity and uncertainty. Sooner or later, people like closure. They grow weary of having to endure open-ended issues, unanswered questions, and a fluid set of responsibilities.

As Woody Allen once said, though, we live in a world with "too many moving parts." So work roles will be a little out of focus much of the time. Careers won't be as cut-and-dried as they used to be. And this is not really happening by choice. The world is forcing our hand.

A rapidly changing world deals ruthlessly with organizations that don't change, and people are coming to respect that fact. For your part, you need to respect the fact that the blur of ambiguity is actually in the best interest of your career. Perpetual change will be crucial if the organization is to survive in the years to come.

This suggests that you should learn to create role clarity *for yourself.* Take personal responsibility for figuring out the top priorities, then point yourself in that direction. Don't pull back, waiting for someone else to happen along who can frame out the specifics of your duties in painstaking detail. Chase down the information you need. Fast. Show initiative in getting your bearings, and in aligning your efforts with the organization's larger plan. Then give yourself permission to attack the job as best you understand it.

Since you'll be going on guesswork to some extent, your ability to tolerate ambiguity and uncertainty will still stand as a "critical skill." So learn to loosen up. Prepare to feel your way along into the future. Be willing to "wing it." Develop your ability to improvise–even reduce it to an art form. And simply accept the fact that your work life is going to be fuzzy around the edges.

Indeed, trying to manage your career will resemble E.L. Doctorow's description of how it feels when writing a book: "It's like driving at night in the fog. You can only see as far as your headlights, but you can make the whole trip that way."

*"The certainty of misery is better than the misery of uncertainty."*
– Pogo comic strip

*Less than half the workforce in the industrial world will be holding conventional full-time jobs in organizations by the beginning of the 21st century. Those full-timers or insiders will be the new minority.*

*Every year more and more people will be self-employed.*

*Many will work temporary or part-time—sometimes because that's the way they want it, sometimes because that's all that is available.*

– Charles Handy
*The Age of Unreason*

# *Behave like you're in business for yourself.*

**Y**our employer wants more than your body, more than just your arms and back and brain. Your employer wants you to act like an *owner.*

Why is this? And what does it really mean?

One reason why you need to think and behave like you're in business for yourself is because organizations are breaking into bits and getting flatter. There's less hierarchy. Fewer layers. The move is toward small scale, decentralized business units–sort of like mini-enterprises, or self-contained work groups–that operate more independently.

Organizations are reshaping themselves in an attempt to become more entrepreneurial. They want to get closer to the customer. They want decisions to be made by the people who are closest to the information. And they want to be able to move *faster.* The idea is that only small units are agile and adaptable enough to thrive in today's world of high-velocity change.

So now we're seeing a lot of self-directed teams. "Empowered" employees. The management ranks are shrinking rapidly, and this means more power, information, and responsibility flow through to you.

You'll need to assume more personal responsibility for the success of the entire enterprise, rather than focusing narrowly within the boundaries of your old job description. To act like an owner you need a sense for managing the whole. You need peripheral vision.

Consider how you–*personally*–can help cut costs, serve the customer better, improve productivity, and innovate. Constantly think in terms of *commercial* success, how you and your group can add directly to the *financial* health of the organization.

This could prove to be more "freedom" than you prefer. For example, if you've found comfort in "working for somebody else"–e.g., having other people call the shots, supervise you, and stand accountable for problems and results–you may start to sweat. On the other hand, behaving like you're in business for yourself gives you the chance to really shine.

Besides all this, though, thinking of yourself as "self-employed" is the mindset that serves *you* best in the years to come. Organizations simply aren't going to look out for people's careers like they did in the past.

Odds are you're on your own. Much like an independent contractor, you have to "build your business," uphold your reputation, and satisfy the people who pay for your work.

So operate as if you're self-employed, and carry personal responsibility for your own career mobility. Whether you look at it from the perspective of your employer, or from the angle that you're a one-person show, it pays to behave like you're in business for yourself.

*"We're all in this alone."*
– Lily Tomlin

*There has been more information produced in the last 30 years than during the previous 5,000.*

*A weekday edition of* The New York Times *contains more information than the average person was likely to come across in a lifetime during 17th-century England.*

*The information supply available to us doubles every 5 years.*

– Richard Saul Wurman
*Information Anxiety*

# *Stay in school.*

**T**oday's world takes no pity on the person who gets lazy about learning. Either you take personal responsibility for continuing your education, or you end up without the knowledge you need to protect your career.

It doesn't take long for skills and knowledge to get outdated in a fast-changing world. Technological advances and the flood of new information make it hard to keep up with what's going on. College graduates can find even their most advanced technical skills outdated in a matter of years. Craftsmen must constantly adapt to new products and techniques. And some careers don't even get a *chance* to change–they simply disappear. We must constantly retool ourselves, become perpetual students, or we risk becoming obsolete.

Lifelong learning is the only way to remain competitive in the job market. You should invest in your own growth, development, and self-renewal. Do this the way a company invests in research and development, and come up with "new and better products or services" you can offer.

Your employer may help out with this, but ultimately the responsibility is yours. Your future "employability"–your appeal as a job candidate–depends on you having a relentless drive to update credentials, acquire new skills, and stay abreast of what's happening in your field.

Homework–studying on your own–should become a regular part of your weekly routine. Read. Attend workshops and seminars. Take courses. Volunteer for understudy or apprentice assignments that let you learn from experts. Accept lateral moves that will broaden you. *Ask* for learning opportunities, and then milk them dry.

It doesn't matter anymore whether you work on cars, teach, farm, or doctor people. You need specialized knowledge. You also need to know how your field or profession is changing. Delve deeper. Keep learning. Be sure to develop transferable skills, too, as this gives "portability" to your career. Don't get locked in to just one job, or even one employer. Give yourself options.

The more you know how to do, and the better you do it, the more valuable you become. The better positioned you are to market yourself. The greater your job security.

So just forget about "finishing" your education. Defend your career by developing a better package of knowledge and skills than the next person.

*"There are two kinds of people, those who finish what they start and so on. . ."*
– Robert Byrne

ENIAC, *commonly thought of as the first modern computer, was built in 1944. It took up more space than an 18-wheeler's tractor trailer, weighed more than 17 Chevrolet Camaros, and consumed 140,000 watts of electricity. ENIAC could execute up to 5,000 basic arithmetic operations per second.*

*One of today's popular microprocessors, the 486, is built on a tiny piece of silicon about the size of a dime. It weighs less than a packet of Sweet 'N Low, and uses less than 2 watts of electricity. A 486 can execute up to 54,000,000 instructions per second.*

*The cost of computing power drops roughly 30% every year, and microchips are doubling in performance power every 18 months.*

– *Business Week*
"The Information Revolution"

*Hold yourself accountable for outcomes.*

**O**rganizations are insisting on new levels of accountability from their employees. Responsibility, power, and authority are being pushed down to the lowest levels. For this to work, you have to stand accountable for results.

Careers simply carry more personal exposure these days. And you can't get off the hook by rationalizing, "I tried...I really worked hard...I did high quality work...I did *my* part." All of those lines sound good on the surface, but they won't sell if the *overall* results aren't there.

In these times of self-directed teams, empowered employees, and "boundaryless" organizations, your worth as an individual employee will also get measured by your work group's collective results.

Holding yourself personally accountable for outcomes requires that you think broadly. Consider the big picture. Look beyond your own immediate behavior–beyond the specifics of your job description–to see if you're really doing all you should to bring about the right results. Learn to work across departmental boundaries. Avoid turf issues. Combine your efforts seamlessly with others who, though very different from you, are contributing to the same end results.

Concentrating on outcomes will also keep you from falling in love with a particular methodology. Or to put it another way, you're less likely to waste time, energy, and other resources on low-payoff work routines if your real passion is for reaching results. Our work processes are always cleanest when we design them to be solely in service of outcomes. So streamline your approach. Eliminate unnecessary steps. Get rid of tasks no one can justify.

The more intent you are on achieving the targeted outcomes, the less tolerant you'll be of clumsy or unnecessary work processes. Having to shoulder personal accountability for results gives you a great incentive to clean out the clutter in how the place operates. The main reason business concepts like "reengineering" and "process improvement" enjoy such popularity today is because organizations are realizing how *approach* can interfere with *outcomes*.

So do your part. Drive the organization directly toward the outcomes that count the most.

*"Somebody has to do something, and it's just incredibly pathetic that it has to be us."*

– Jerry Garcia of The Grateful Dead

*Let's say you're going to a party, so you pull out some pocket change and buy a little greeting card that plays "Happy Birthday" when it's opened. After the party, someone casually tosses the card into the trash, throwing away more computer power than existed in the entire world before 1950.*

*The home video camera you use to take pictures of the party contains more processing power than an old IBM 360, the wonder machine that gave birth to the mainframe computer age.*

*The party gift you give is a system called Saturn, made by Sega, the gamemaker. It runs on a higher-performance processor than the original 1976 Cray supercomputer, which in its day was accessible to only the most elite physicists.*

– John Huey
"Waking Up to the New Economy"
*Fortune,* June 27, 1994

43

# *Add value.*

**M**ake sure you contribute more than you cost. Employees often mislead themselves, assuming they should get to keep their jobs if they're responsible and do good work. Some of them even have the idea that sticking around for a long time makes them worth more to the organization.

Of course, experience may count for something. But maybe not. It depends on whether that experience really makes you worth more to your employer today, or whether it has mainly lost all value because the world is changing so rapidly.

The "loyalty" issue is a little stickier. People who have shown true devotion over the years–those who have hung in there during tough times and truly worked from the heart–should get points for that. No question, that's a real virtue. That's valuable stuff.

We must realize, however, that we can use history to justify our continued employment for only so long. We still need to add value *now*. And we should not confuse *longevity* with *loyalty*. The mere fact that a person has been on the payroll for years says nothing. You don't get points for just "putting in your time."

It's your *contribution* that counts. Not the hours (or years) you put in. Or how busy you are.

We've all seen people who stay busy–who even work hard–without adding any real value. They make the mistake of thinking effort should earn them a paycheck. You can respect them for trying, but you can't justify the cost of keeping them on board. Their careers are built on make-believe.

You'll be better off if you think in terms of being paid for performance–for the value you add–rather than for your tenure, good intentions, or activity level. Prove your worth to the organization. Make a difference. Add enough value so everyone can see that something very important would be missing if you left.

"*The factory of the future will have only two employees, a man and a dog. The man will be there to feed the dog. The dog will be there to keep the man from touching the equipment.*"

– Warren Bennis

Author and Distinguished
Professor of Business Administration,
University of Southern California

*The first practical industrial robot was introduced during the 1960's.*

*By 1982 there were approximately 32,000 robots being used in the United States.*

*Today there are over 20,000,000.*

## *See yourself as a service center.*

Your job security depends on how valuable you are to your "customers." The better you serve them, the better you protect your career.

This heightens the importance of knowing precisely who these people are. You need an in-depth feel for your targeted market. What do your customers do, and how do you fit into the picture? What are their needs? What does it take to please them? How can you contribute to their success?

Sharpen your insights into your personal "marketplace," and you'll see exactly what you should do to make yourself indispensable.

Keep in mind that there are both *internal* and *external* customers. You may deal directly with each type, but let's focus on whom you're supposed to serve *inside* the organization. It may be some other department, several people in your own functional area, or just your direct supervisor. Maybe you've always thought of them as coworkers, or as people you work *with* rather than *for*. But make no mistake–these are your clients and customers.

Too often we don't stop and think about the full implications of this. We more or less take our jobs for granted. This means we're taking our customers for granted, and that's a risky way to run a career.

Unless you take pains to provide the best possible service, and do so at a competitive market price (i.e., salary), you'll find it hard to keep customers. They'll replace you with a better service provider. In essence, somebody else will "steal your business."

The more you allow your service to go soft, the greater the odds you could end up in some downsizing statistics. Or, the organization might simply decide to outsource your work, to farm it out to some other firm that specializes in doing what you do. More than likely, you're actually in competition with external providers who offer the same service, whether you realize it or not. Question is, who will provide the best bargain, you or somebody else?

You must get close–intimately close–to your customers. Seek regular, direct contact with them. Build a strong relationship. Deliver the highest quality service possible. Anticipate their needs, and develop a reputation for responsiveness.

In the final analysis, customers are your only source of job security.

*"They laughed at Joan of Arc, but she went right ahead and built it."*
– Gracie Allen

*Development of the integrated circuit (invented in the late 1950's) has permitted an ever-increasing amount of information to be processed or stored on a single microchip. This is what has driven the Information Revolution.*

*Between 1960 and 1970, the number of components on a chip doubled each year from 1 in 1960 to 1,000 in 1970. Since then the number of components has doubled every year and a half, reaching 100,000,000 in 1990 and 1,000,000,000 in 1992.*

*Today's average consumers wear more computing power on their wrists than existed in the entire world before 1961.*

– Ian Morrison and Greg Schmid
*Future Tense: The Business Realities of the Next Ten Years*

## *Manage your own morale.*

**S**omehow, over the years, we've been led to believe that higher management is accountable for employee morale. Nobody even seems to question this notion anymore. If attitudes go sour, the boss gets the blame. If employees are mentally down and out, the company is expected to provide emotional hand-holding until its people are happy again.

We've got to get past a lot of this nonsense, because *nobody* is well-served by this line of reasoning.

Sure, the way the place is being run, and the way people get treated, are factors employees must reckon with. But let's give the average individual a lot more credit for being able to manage his or her own morale. If we attribute more emotional self-sufficiency to people–if we *expect* ourselves to stand personally responsible for our attitudes–we'll all be much better off.

Saddling someone else with the job of keeping you contented and upbeat at work is a slick move. And it may even seem justified if we warp our logic a little bit. After all, organizations actually do treat people unfairly at times. And some managers are jerks. But overall, employees don't seem to deserve any higher marks for how *they* treat employers. And since the world at large displays no concept of "fairness" in the way it deals with organizations, sometimes companies are forced into corners. Higher management can end up *having* to do things that are hard for people to accept. This doesn't mean that whoever is in charge should carry the burden of responsibility to pump you back up and give you a positive attitude.

If you put someone else in charge of your morale,

you disempower yourself. If you wait around for higher management to heal your wounded spirit, you'll end up hurting longer than necessary.

You're far better off to assign yourself personal responsibility for attitude control. Don't let low morale drain away precious energy, destroy your self-confidence, or damage your attractiveness as a job candidate. Organizations want employees who can cope with change without breaking stride. So take charge of your moods. *Act* upbeat, and you start to *feel* better. Show resilience–bounce back on your own–rather than allowing yourself to wallow in negative emotions such as anger, depression, or grief.

Sure, grieving over personal loss is natural. Sometimes it's a necessary part of the recovery process. But some people adopt it as a lifestyle, become martyrs, and lick their wounds for the rest of their careers. Frankly, giving in to grief has limited healing power, and you need to get beyond it.

Rapid organizational change guarantees us that almost everybody is going to carry some battle scars in the years to come. You can be bitter about how your career gets affected, or you can demonstrate your ability to take a punch. You can carry a grudge to your grave, or you can "get over it."

What's best for your career? Depersonalize the situation–accept it as the luck of the draw–and harbor no resentment toward higher management. Ideally, you'll accept change as an exercise that, though sometimes painful, helps you build more emotional muscle.

*"If a cat spoke, it would say things like, 'Hey, I don't see the* problem *here.'"*
– Roy Blount, Jr.

*Computer power is now 8,000 times less expensive than it was 30 years ago.*

*Randall Tobias, former Vice Chairman of AT&T, offers this comparison to explain the astounding rate of advancement in computerization:*

"If we had similar progress in automotive technology, today you could buy a Lexus for about $2. It would travel at the speed of sound, and go about 600 miles on a thimble of gas."

– John Naisbitt
*Global Paradox*

# *Practice* kaizen.

**A** strong organization is in the best position to protect your career. If it's financially successful, your paycheck is more secure. If it keeps getting better and better in the way it does business, your future usually gets brighter.

But the organization can't improve unless its people do.

Continuous improvement—the Japanese call it *kaizen*—offers some of the best insurance for both your career and the organization. *Kaizen* (pronounced ky´zen) is the relentless quest for a better way, for higher quality craftsmanship. Think of it as the daily pursuit of perfection.

*Kaizen* keeps you reaching, stretching to outdo yesterday. The continuous improvements may come bit by bit. But enough of these small, incremental gains will eventually add up to a valuable competitive advantage. Also, if every employee constantly keeps an eye out for improvements, major innovations are more likely to occur. The spirit of *kaizen* can trigger dramatic breakthroughs.

Without *kaizen*, you and your employer will gradually lose ground. Eventually, you'll both be "out of business," because the competition never stands still.

Tom Peters puts it this way: "Good quality is a stupid idea. The only thing that counts is your quality getting better at a more rapid rate than your principal competitors. It's real simple. If we're not getting more, better, faster than *they* are getting more, better, faster, then we're getting less better or more worse."

*Nobody* can afford to rest on a reputation anymore. Circumstances change too quickly. Competition gets tougher and more global all the time. What we consider "good" today is seen as "so-so" by tomorrow.

Every single employee should assume personal responsibility for upgrading his or her job performance. Your productivity, response time, quality, cost control, and customer service should all show steady gains. And your skills should be in a state of constant renewal.

Granted, this drive toward an ever-improving performance doesn't guarantee job security, raises, or promotions. You still can be a victim of circumstances, even in strong, financially successful organizations. But if you've passionately practiced *kaizen*, you'll have built your competency level. Your track record will help sell you. So you'll at least find it easier to resume your career in another setting.

"*The first time I walked into a trophy shop, I looked around and thought to myself, 'This guy is good!'*"
– Fred Wolf

*In 1991, nearly 1 out of 3 American workers had been with their employer for less than a year, and almost 2 out of 3 for less than 5 years.*

*The United States' contingent workforce—consisting of roughly 45,000,000 temporaries, self-employed, part-timers, or consultants—has grown 57% since 1980.*

*Going, if not yet gone, are the 9-5 workdays, lifetime jobs, predictable, hierarchical relationships, corporate culture security blankets, and, for a large and growing sector of the work-force, the workplace itself (replaced by a cybernetics "workspace").*

*Constant training, retraining, job-hopping, and even career-hopping, will become the norm.*

– Mary O'Hara-Devereaux
and Robert Johansen

*GlobalWork:
Bridging Distance,
Culture and Time*

# *Be a fixer, not a finger-pointer.*

**P**roblems are the natural offspring of change, so you'll see plenty of them in the years to come. Build a name for yourself as a problem-solver, and you'll be a valuable person to have around.

Organizations need people who can take care of problems, not merely point them out. Too many employees get this confused. They seem to think complaining is a constructive act. They're keen on identifying all the problems–often in an accusing, blaming fashion–but contribute little toward improving things. Their attitude is, "Upper management is supposed to make it all work. We'll sit back, watch them struggle, and second-guess their solutions."

As employees–in fact, as an entire society–we've gotten unbelievably good at the blame game. We're experts at dodging personal responsibility and using our energy to criticize and complain instead. This carries a terrific cost. So long as we search beyond ourselves for solutions, we disempower ourselves. You might say that even as we commit the crime and blame somebody else, we also become the victim.

Even when we find someone else to blame for our circumstances, we win a hollow victory. It may feel good for the moment to get ourselves off the hook, but it perpetuates the problem.

Finger-pointing does not position us to do our part–that only *we* can do–toward workable solutions.

We've come to expect too much of our institutions, and too little of ourselves as individuals. In the long haul, it simply doesn't work. The organization's values grow out of individual employees' values. The organization's results are merely the accumulation of singular people's results.

So instead of being a finger-pointer, and rather than trying to single out somebody to blame, assume ownership of problems. Let the solutions start with you. You'll increase your odds of career success.

*"We have only one person to blame, and that's each other."*

– Barry Beck,
New York Ranger, on
who started a brawl
during the NHL's
Stanley Cup playoffs

Look at a roster of the 100 largest U.S. companies at the beginning of the 1900's. You'll find that only 16 are still in existence.

Then consider Fortune *magazine's* first list (published in 1956) of America's 500 biggest companies. Only 29 out of the 100 firms topping that first "Fortune 500" could still be found in the top 100 by 1992.

*During the decade of the 1980's, a total of 230 companies—46%—disappeared from the "Fortune 500."*

*Obviously, size does not guarantee continued success. Neither does a good reputation.*

# *Alter your expectations.*

Organizations can't stop the world from changing. The best they can do is adapt. The smart ones change before they have to. The lucky ones manage to scramble and adjust when push comes to shove. The rest are losers, and they become history.

As organizations maneuver in an effort to cope with rapid change, some careers always get caught in the cracks. It's unfortunate, but unavoidable. Some employees get pinched and, naturally, people cry foul. They accuse top management of "breaking the psychological contract," of changing the rules. But it's more accurate to say the organization is merely responding to a rule change called by the *world*. The irony is that executives are in a no-win situation. If they're smart, and change early like they should, they're described as uncaring and over-reactive. If they drag around and don't change until the world forces the issue, they're considered inept as well as cruel.

Part of the problem lies in the "entitlement" mindset that has crept into our thinking over the past several decades. People came to believe that, because of all the years of work they put in, the organization "owed" them continued employment. Sticking with an outfit–loosely referred to as loyalty–was supposed to entitle a person to job security. Employees learned to expect regular pay increases and periodic promotions. Some folks even went so far as to presume they had a "right" to expect their employers to keep them happy and provide high job satisfaction. The burden of responsibility for people's careers kept shifting further and further away from employees, and more onto the backs of employers. Both parties bought into this system, and it has been bad for all concerned. Too often employees rested on their past achievements, instead of requiring themselves to constantly upgrade their skills. They counted on their work *history* to qualify them for a promising career *future*. They became too dependent on their employers, expecting protective employee policies to shield them from the raw forces of change going on around the globe.

Obviously, it didn't work. High-velocity change has eliminated the need for many jobs. Because of new technology and global competition, organizations are being reshaped and work is being done differently. The marketplace is merciless, and it puts definite limits on how generous or protective an organization can be with its people.

This means you should reframe your

relationship with the organization, just as it must reframe its relationship with customers and competitors. Don't fall into the trap of assuming that you're automatically "entitled" to pay increases, promotions, or even your job...*even if you perform well.* Circumstances will keep changing. The best thing you can do is constantly upgrade your skills, stay flexible, and never con yourself into thinking that your employer is supposed to protect your future.

The era of entitlement is ending. Instead of relying on your "rights," take personal responsibility for your career. Put your faith in the future...and in yourself. Embrace change, and develop the work habits you need for job success in the Information Age.

*"It's a question of whether we're going to go forward into the future, or past to the back."*

– Vice President Dan Quayle

# Books By PRITCHETT & ASSOCIATES, INC.

*Resistance: Moving Beyond the Barriers to Change*

* *Mergers: Growth in the Fast Lane*

* *A Survival Guide to the Stress of Organizational Change*

* *Firing Up Commitment During Organizational Change*

* *The Employee Handbook of New Work Habits for a Radically Changing World*

*The Team Member Handbook for Teamwork*

* *Culture Shift: The Employee Handbook for Changing Corporate Culture*

* *High-Velocity Culture Change: A Handbook for Managers*

*The Quantum Leap Strategy*

*you$^2$: A High Velocity Formula for Multiplying your Personal Effectiveness in Quantum Leaps*

*The Ethics of Excellence*

*The Employee Survival Guide to Mergers and Acquisitions*

*After the Merger: Managing the Shockwaves*

*Making Mergers Work: A Guide to Managing Mergers and Acquisitions*

*Service Excellence!*

* *Business As UnUsual: The Handbook for Managing and Supervising Organizational Change*

* *The Employee Handbook for Organizational Change*

* *Team ReConstruction: Building A High Performance Work Group During Change*

*Smart Moves: A Crash Course on Merger Integration Management*

* *Training programs also available. Please call 1-800-622-8989 for more information.*

*Call 214-789-7999 for information regarding international rights and foreign translations.*

## If You Like This Handbook, You'll *Love* This Training Program!

# NEW WORK HABITS FOR A RADICALLY CHANGING WORLD

*Quick-Impact Training Program for Managers and Employees*

*New Work Habits* literally corners us with the reality of how we must change because of the radical shifts in the world around us. It uses a blend of lecturettes, group and individual discovery exercises, and open discussions to drive home the powerful points that Price Pritchett makes in this handbook.

The *employee* version of *New Work Habits* is taught in a 4-hour format, while the *manager's* version is 6 hours in length. Both programs contain the following modules:

MODULE I: Meet Hard Reality Head-On

MODULE II: Build Your Capability

MODULE III: Build Your Commitment

The *manager's* version also contains a crucial fourth component based on the companion handbook, *Firing Up Commitment During Organizational Change*. MODULE IV focuses managers on creating a work environment conducive to their employees' development of the "new work habits."

Call **1-800-622-8989** for more information.

# Management Consulting Services

Pritchett & Associates developed its in-depth expertise by working with Fortune 500 clients for over 20 years. The key to our success is an intimate understanding of organizations undergoing major change. We combine extensive, "hands-on" executive experience with an analytic, results-oriented approach to problem solving. Our consultants have the know-how to:

- Exploit instability rather than merely cope with change
- Assess your culture, organization, and management processes to develop high-impact change initiatives
- Move you from plans to accomplishments...to become an adaptive organization
- Apply leading edge change management expertise and merger integration services to your critical business challenges

# Training Programs to Implement Change

Pritchett training programs build on the hard-hitting principles in our best-selling handbooks. These quick-impact, concentrated programs deliver a no-nonsense message on how to deal with today's rapidly changing business environment. Our training helps your organization:

- Accept—not resist—the predictable dynamics of change
- Underline why every employee must become a change agent
- Get people to take personal responsibility for making change work
- Protect—and even improve—operating efficiency and productivity
- Learn to communicate change effectively
- Keep employees focused on the "high-priority" issues—your business and your customers
- Recognize and capitalize on the opportunities created by change.